This

the beautiful Frideswide (c. 735), that young lady, wise beyond her years, who anticipating marriage to a savage bore, similar to many littering these 16 pages, refused queenship, preferring a life of contemplative virginity in a pigsty at Binsey Abbey.

Jane Shore

Adelaide (d. 1848 aged 57), 26 year old German bride of 53 year old William IV. After two infant children died she was very fond of her niece, Victoria.

Adeliza of Louvain (d. 1151 aged 48), a tranquil beautiful homebody married at 15 to 50 year old widower, Henry II. Her true passion was needlework but she bore 7 children to her second husband, Albini.

Aethelflaed (c. 960), the White Duck, King Edgar's exquisite concubine.

Agatha (c. 1060), wife of Edgar the Atheling, rightful but rejected king.

Alexandra of Denmark (d. 1925 aged 80), an unpunctual, auburn-haired, blue-eyed beauty married at 18 to Edward VII and mother of 6 children. With advancing years came deafness and dignified indifference to her husband's infidelity.

Algitha (c. 1016), a Danish widow who first married Edmund Ironside and then arranged his murder by her brother.

Algiva (c. 1020), 1st wife of Canute. It is said that, being barren, her two children were changeling sons of a nun and of a cobbler. After being put away she married King Harald Harefoot (Hairylegs).

Algytha (c. 1050), enchanting wife of Gruffydd the Welshman, seized and wed by King Harold after the defeat and death of her husband.

Alice Perrers (d. 1400), wife of William Perrers, the notorious mistress of Edward III in his dotage. She insisted on sitting with judges trying cases in which she was the defendant and stripped the most valuable rings from the fingers of the dying king.

Alwitha (c. 901), wife of Alfred the Great and lost in his shadow.

Anne (d. 1714 aged 48), daughter of James II, married George of Denmark, an overweight virile glutton who sired her 18 children, none surviving infancy. She was a dull person, usually unwell and often uncharitable. Her farming levy, much resented by non-Anglicans, made parsons rich for 200 years.

Anne of Bohemia (d. 1394, aged 28, of the plague), sister of Good King Wenceslaus. Because of a budget deficit regalia was pawned to pay for her wedding at 14 to teenage Richard II. She introduced side-saddle riding and a 2 feet tall fashion in hats.

Anne of Cleves (d. 1557 aged 42), could not speak English when she became 4th wife of Henry VIII, deluded by a flattering Holbein portrait. Before a swift divorce he called her his 'Flemish Mare' and, afterwards, his 'sister'.

Anne Boleyn (d. 1536, aged 29, of judicial murder), a Kent girl, was pregnant when she became Henry VIII's second wife. After birth of Elizabeth (later queen) only a male heir could have saved her from her abominable husband. On a trumped up charge of adultery she was beheaded without blindfold by a French swordsman.

Anne of Denmark (d. 1619 aged 45, of dropsy), an attractive, empty-headed blonde who, at 15, married James VI/I, Mary, Queen of Scots' son who, although he preferred good-looking young men, fathered 7 children.

Anne Hyde (d. 1671 aged 34, of breast cancer), plain, lively daughter of historian Clarendon who, as dowry, handed over Hyde Park. She was pregnant when Charles II ordered his brother, later James II, to marry her and, using a curtain ring, the ceremony took place in the middle of the night. Charles usually called his brother 'Tom Otter', a henpecked character in a play.

Anne Neville (d. 1485 aged 29, of consumption) was married unwillingly to Richard III, Crouchback, who, in cold blood, had butchered the Prince of Wales, her fiance, after the Battle of Tewkesbury. She, her husband and son died within a year.

Audrey (d. 674), was a widow when she wed King Egfrid of Northumbria, yet remained a virgin until death. She became Abbess of Ely and, to mortify the flesh, took a bath three times a year.

Avice of Gloucester (b. 1167), the 1st wife of King John was divorced for consanguinity but, true to form, he kept the dowry. Her 2nd husband was Geoffrey de Mandeville and her sister is the only Mabel to make the history books.

Barbara Villiers (d. 1709 aged 68), ravishingly lovely wife of Mr. Palmer and the sexually greedy money-grabbing mistress of Charles II to whom she bore 5 children, (the Countess of Surrey, Duke of Southampton, Duke of Grafton, Countess of Lichfield and Duke of Northumberland). She had a daughter by the Duke of Marlborough, Victor of Blenheim and a son by Mr. Goodman, an actor. She earned the titles of Countess of Castlemaine and Duchess of Cleveland.

Berengaria of Navarre, daughter of King Sancho the Wise, married Richard Coeur de Lion on Cyprus. He thus avoided marrying a Frenchwoman who, he claimed had a son by his father but was made to pay a large fine for 'using' her. Berengaria never came to England but, much later, a Cunard liner was named after her.

Bertha (d. 616), daughter of the King of Paris, an affable, condescending beauty who charmed her spouse, Ethelbert, King of Kent, into inviting the evangelist, Augustine, who unexpectedly converted him.

Boadicea (d. 60 A.D. of poisoning), widow Queen of East Anglia who, after suffering a public whipping and the ravishing of her daughters, exacted a terrible revenge on 80,000 Roman colonists around Colchester

Caroline of Brunswick (d. 1821 aged 53, of emotional distress), wife of George IV ('Prinny'), who refused her admission to the Coronation because she hadn't a ticket.

Cartifin-Andera, Queen of the Brigantes, betrayed Caractacus, put away her failing husband and married a teenage squire.

Caroline of Brandenburg-Anspach (d. 1737 aged 53, of a woman's complaint), a brave, sensible woman, handsome in the German style. For years she hid an umbilical rupture for fear of losing her husband, George II but, at the same time, cooling his passions by, for instance, substituting on his bedroom wall a Van Dyck portrait for a Rubens' bouncing nude. As she lay dying she urged him to remarry but, weeping bitterly, he answered, 'Non, j'aurai de maitresses.' 'Ah!' she murmured, 'Cela non empeche pas.'

Catherine of Aragon (d. 1536 aged 51) daughter of Ferdinand & Isabella, was married at 16 to the 14 year old Prince of Wales, but they were kept well apart and he died prematurely. Her mother forbade her to marry her late boy-husband's father, Henry VII. After marriage to Henry VIII only one of her 6 children lived (later Queen Mary). After the cruel divorce (which founded the Church of England) the odious tyrant slowly pauperised her but did not break her spirit.

Catherine of Braganza (d. 1705 aged 67), a simple Portuguese with a dowry of £5 million, married at 24 to the philanderer Charles II whose highest praise of her was, 'There isn't anything in her face to actually shock one.' She suffered his dispersed harem with dignity.

Catherine Howard (d. 1542 aged 19, of royal murder), daughter of the Victor of Flodden Field, a high-spirited, irresponsible girl, Henry VIII's 5th wife. Her indiscretions were reported by Archbishop Cranmer and her lovers racked into confession. She was killed without trial.

Catherine Parr (d. 1548 aged 36, of puerperal fever), a spirited little woman, 6th wife of Henry VIII who was her third husband. Marriage to this axe-happy, ulcerated, impotent monster was a nightmare but she survived it to triumphantly lead a 4th husband to the altar.

Catherine of Valois (d. 1437 aged 36), daughter of the French King, wife of Henry V, Victor of Agincourt. After his death she married secretly Owen Tudor, a Welshman and the handsomest man of his time. When, in the 17th Century, her body was disinterred Samuel Pepys kissed her forehead on his birthday.

Cendrith (c. 600), wife of Cedwalla, King of Wessex, who rounded up the entire savage population of the Isle of Wight and with a brigade of armed evangelists, baptised them in a single day.

Charlotte—Sophia of Mecklenburg-Strelitz (d. 1818 aged 73), a thin chattering brunette who devotedly saw her husband, George III through several spells of derangement.

Cinefwintha (c. 655), daughter of Penda the Pagan, after being taken in good faith by King Offa of Essex, persuaded him to become a monk.

Clementina Walkenshaw (c. 1750) mistress of Prince Charles Edward and alleged to have been a Hanoverian spy.

Ealdgyth of Northampton (c. 1030), from the age of 15 to 50 said to be the most desirable woman in England, in rotation, was mistress to King Olaf the Saint, wife to King Edmund, King Edwy the Fair, King Ethelred the Unready and King Canute's paramour. This voluptuous creature was almost equal to the acknowledged sexual

insatiability of King Edwy but, at times, was forced to recruit her mother. The Archbishop of Canterbury had to drag this satyr from bed where he lay between the two to compel attendance at his own coronation. After her husband's death the Church punished her for her sins by excommunication, branding, hamstringing and, finally, sending her to Northern Ireland. Because of alternative spellings of her name less scrupulous biographers have confused her with several other women.

Edelburga (c. 799), having poisoned her husband, King Brithnic of Wessex, fled to a French monastery but was turned out after being surprised with an English gentleman. She died of want in Pavia.

Edgwa (d. 924), 3rd wife of Edward the Elder. Two sons became kings.

Editha (d. 1075), Earl Godwin's daughter, wife of Edward the Confessor who, it is said did not consummate the union as a test of his virtue against temptation. She abolished the custom of allowing bishops and abbots to be kissed by ladies.

Edith of the Swan-neck, the elegant and faithful paramour of King Harold to whom she presented 5 children. After the Battle of Hastings she identified his body by birth marks known only to her and arranged his burial in Waltham Abbey.

Egwina (c. 910), 1st wife of Edward the Elder, was a simple but personable shepherd's daughter who dreamed that the moon shone from her womb and lit all England. Her husband is said to have loved her with a violent passion. She was the mother of King Athelstan.

Eleanor of Aquitaine (d. 1204 aged 82), a fierce women's libber divorced by the King of France married Henry II and had 9 children. She is said to have arranged the murder of his beautiful mistress, Fair Rosamund.

Eleanor of Castille (d. 1290) of a fever) was married at 10 to Edward I, Longshanks, the Hammer of the Scots, and bore 13 children usually whilst on campaign, including the first English Prince of Wales. Her bowels are buried at Lincoln. Crosses were set up at each spot where her bier rested on her corpse's journey to Westminster.

Eleanor of Provence (d. 1291 at Amesbury), la Belle, wife of Henry III, bore 13 children. She was hated by London merchants because of her commercial interests. She died a nun.

Elfgifu of Northampton, believed by some to be EALD-GYTH (see above).

Elfleda the Fair (970), mistress then wife of Edgar the Peaceful, supplanting a nun.

Elfthryth (c. 975), her electrifying beauty so stunned the king's marriage guidance counsellor that he returned a nil report and married her. However truth leaked and, on the eve of King Edgar the Peaceful's personal inspection, she was begged on knees to defuse her explosive charms. Contrarily she shone more radiantly and the king personally slew her husband, and married the widow. After Edgar's death she superintended the stabbing of her step-son, Edward the Martyr at Corfe. She ended her days in a nunnery, her body covered with painted crosses to fend off the Devil. So they say.

Elgiva (c. 955), wife of Edwy the Fair, sometimes confused with EALDGYTH (see above).

Elgiva (c. 945), wife of King Edmund, a violent young man who was stabbed to his death whilst arresting an outlaw who had insinuated himself into a festal party. Some people say she also was EALDGYTH (see above).

Elizabeth Bowes-Lyon (b. 1900) married George VI and has two children.

Elizabeth Windsor, Elizabeth II (b. 1926), married Philip Mountbatten and has 4 children.

Elizabeth Talbot claimed to have been married to Edward IV by the Bishop of Bath & Wells. She had 2 children.

Elizabeth Tudor, the First (d. 1603 aged 69, of pneumonia), Gloriana, was 3 when her mother was beheaded, at 22 was imprisoned in the Tower and at 59 was saved from smallpox by a German. She was a dancing addict, swore, drank, spat and wrote enchanting letters. In later life her teeth turned black. She had the rare quality of enlisting the loyalty of unusually gifted men. Parliament often vainly petitioned her to marry but whether she really was a Virgin Queen we shall never know.

> *Tandis qu'* Elizabeth *fut Roy,*
> L' Anglois *fut d'* Espagne *l' effroy,*
> *Maintenant, devise et caquette,*
> *Regi par la Reine Jaquette.*
>
> That is literally in *English.*
>
> *Whilst* Elizabeth *was* King,
> The English *were of* Spain *the Terror*
> But now, *governed by* Queen James:
> *They only talk and prattle.*

Elizabeth of York (d. 1503 aged 38 in childbirth) is the queen on playing cards, wife of Henry VII, her second husband. Her wedding carpet was torn up by souvenir hunters before she set foot on it. When her eldest son, Arthur, died she told the king, 'God is where he was and we are both young enough'.

Elizabeth Woodville (d. 1492 aged 54), a Northamptonshire silver-blonde beauty, whose second husband was Edward IV. She said that she was too lowly to be his wife but too proud to be his concubine. She had 10 children, including the Princes in the Tower and the wife of Henry VII. Until he died of gastronomic, alcoholic and sexual excess, she shared him with 3 regular mistresses who he claimed were the wisest, wittiest and holiest women in England.

Emma (d. 1052), The Pearl of Normandy, 2nd wife of Ethelred the Unready and also of Canute who was 10 years her junior. She was wife to two kings and mother of four kings, an all-time record. But an equally remarkable triumph awaited old age when, to prove innocence, she walked barefoot over nine red-hot ploughshares without scorching.

Ethelburga (c. 625), 2nd wife of Edwin of Northumbria, converted the Yorkshire Pagans with the aid of an evangelist, Paulinus.

Guinevere (see Lord Tennyson also Thos. Malory).

Henrietta Maria (d. 1669 aged 60, of an over-draught), a plucky, vivacious French princess married at 15 to Charles I, called by some 'Saint' and others, 'a brave stubborn solemn prig'. Returning from a gun-running expedition she landed at Bridlington under fire.

Isabella of Angouleme (d. 1246), abducted at 13 and married to King John, her second husband. She thirdly married her daughter's fiance whose father had enjoyed her (if you can work that out). She had four pairs of boots and stayed in bed until noon reading romances. She was a great beauty.

Isabella of France (d. 1358, aged 65), Shakespeare's 'she wolf', a very amorous woman wasted on Edward II who gave her wedding presents to him to men friends. Helped by Lord Mortimer, she imprisoned her husband and arranged his murder by inserting a red hot wire into his bowels through a horn tube (so as to leave no mark). Her son, Edward III killed her lover and she died demented.

Jane Grey (d. 1554 aged 19, of judicial murder), The Nine Days Queen, a Leicestershire girl who knew several languages. She was a victim of her father-in-law's ambition and, on her way to the block, passed the headless body of her young husband.

Jane Seymour (d. 1537 aged 28, after childbirth), 3rd wife of Henry VIII and mother of Edward VI. She was a Wiltshire girl.

Jane Shore (c. 1475), wife of a London merchant and long-lying mistress of Edward IV. After death withdrew his protection she was made to do penance in a shift holding a candle.

Joanna of Navarre (d. 1437 aged 67), daughter of Charles the Mad, a widow with 8 children who married Henry IV.

Judith (c. 853) daughter of Charles the Bald, at the age of 12 married Ethelwulf, who already had 5 children and one natural son (an Oxford don). She later married a stepson and, still later, was abducted by Baldwin Ironhand, a Flemish thug.

Louisa of Stolberg (m. 1772), wife of Prince Charles Edward (known to some as Charles III) but left him after suffering drunken beatings. She had a daughter, Clementina.

Louise Keroualle (d. 1734 aged 85) combined the offices of maitresse en titre to Charles II and Maid of Honour to his sister. As a reward for satisfactory service she was made Duchess of Portsmouth and her son, the Duke of Richmond.

Margaret of Anjou (d. 1482 aged 53, of want), ruled her husband, Henry VI who gave her a lion as a wedding present. Her only son was killed at the Battle of Tewkesbury.

Margaret of France (d. 1318 aged 35), married at 18 to 60 year old Edward I, father of her 3 children. She died at Marlborough. A stone carving at Winchelsea shows her to have been a raving beauty.

Maria Clementina Sobieski (m. 1719), Polish wife of James Edward, said by some to be James III and by others, The Old Pretender, a supposititious baby. After 5 years of marriage to this 'tame, flabby fellow who laughed like an idiot', she took the veil.

Maria Fitzherbert (d. 1837 aged 80), secretly married her 3rd husband, George IV at her own house.

Mary Bohun (d. 1394), a great heiress, 1st wife of Henry IV and mother of 6 children.

Mary of Modena (d. 1718 aged 61), 2nd wife of James II who was old enough to be her father. 4 of her 6 children died in infancy and, to discredit his claim to the throne, her sole surviving male child was said by the Whigs to have been insinuated into her curtained bed in a warming-pan and, therefore, supposititious.

Mary Stuart (d. 1694 aged 32, of smallpox), daughter of James II and wife of William of Orange, a sensitive, intelligent woman whose death sent her husband into frightening paroxysms of grief.

Mary of Teck (d. 1953) married George V. She had 6 children.

Mary Tudor (d. 1558 aged 42) daughter of Catherine of Aragon, Mary I. Her marriage to Philip of Spain alarmed English Protestants and nationalists. She mistook a tumour for pregnancy and died deserted and embittered. 'You will find Calais written on my heart' is the best known remark in English history.

Matilda (d. 1118), wife of Henry I. Despite her aunt's whippings she refused to wear a black veil. Later however, this spirited girl became a great friend of the poor, washing the ulcerated feet of the untalented and by Arts Council type grants salving the bruised egos of artists and writers.

Matilda of Flanders (d. 1083 aged 51), who having been spurned by a handsome Saxon had him imprisoned for life after her marriage to William the Conqueror. After an unkind remark about his illegitimacy he beat her whilst still engaged, but their marriage was happy and she bore 9 children. She gave the Bayeux Tapestry to Caen Abbey.

Nell Gwynne, a ravishing fruiterer, mistress of Charles II and thus mother of the 1st Duke of St. Albans.

Matilda of Boulogne (d. 1152 aged 45), the loyal, brave wife of King Stephen.

Osburh (c. 830), 1st wife of Ethelwulf and mother of Alfred the Great.

Philippa of Hainault (d. 1369 aged 55 of dropsy), married at 14 to Edward III had a 'full feminine shape' and bore 12 children. She not only saved the Burghers of Calais but also some English carpenters whose platform collapsed under the king whilst opening a Buy British Trade Fair in France. She introduced Flemish weavers to East Anglia.

Quindrida (c. 757) wife of Offa (of the Dyke).

Redburga (c. 838), the swooningly lovely racialist wife of Egbert who she persuaded to ban Welsh immigration. (see Offa)

Rosamund Clifford (d. 1116), Henry II's passionately loved paramour who he kept hid in a Woodstock maze so complicated that a silken thread was needed to unravel it. Some say that the queen gave her a choice of dagger or poison but it is more likely that she died naturally at Godstow. An old-fashioned rose is named after her.

Rowena (c. 475), a pagan Jutish beauty who was given to King Vortigern by her uncles, Hengist & Horsa, in exchange for Kent.

Sexburga (c. 627), sole queen of Wessex, 'a woman of courage, subtle and extensive genius', an early victim of sex-discrimination, being deposed because her nobles refused to accept her orders.

Sophia Dorothea of Celle (m. 1682), cousin and wife of George I, was imprisoned by him for life whilst he enjoyed two huge mistresses known to Londoners as the Elephant and Castle.

Victoria (d. 1901 aged 81), married Albert of Saxe-coburg-Gotha and had 9 children. She gave her name to an Age.